MW01155098

Short Row Tunisian Fashion

6

9

12

17

22

25

LEISURE ARTS, INC. • Little Rock, Arkansas

What is a Short Row?

Short rows are used for shaping by adding height to a piece. In this book the short rows form wedges, which will add height to either the beginning or the end of a piece.

In Tunisian crochet there are many different ways to make a short row. This book includes two different techniques.

The first short row technique (Technique 1) is to work across the row on the forward pass to within a few stitches before the end, leaving the remaining stitches unworked, then close. Each subsequent row is a few stitches less until there are only a few stitches remaining. This will add height at the beginning of the piece and will form a wedge. If you continue working the technique, you will form a circle, such as the Body of the Triangles Beret on page 6, which can be seamed.

The second short row technique (Technique 2) is worked during the return pass in which only a few stitches are closed each time with the number of stitches being closed increasing with each short row worked. This will add height at the end of the piece and will form a wedge.

Are all Short Rows the same?

When you alternate both techniques, the edges of the piece will be straight, as shown in the Triangles Scarf on page 9.

The height of a short row wedge can be varied by changing the number of unworked stitches. The wedge shown below was worked by leaving 2 stitches unworked on the forward passes *(Fig. 1)*.

Fig. 1

The wedge shown below was worked by leaving 6 stitches unworked on the forward passes *(Fig. 2)*.

Fig. 2

Both wedges begin with the same number of stitches, but the second wedge is not as tall because it had fewer short rows.

Making a Short Row

There are two short row techniques you need to learn to complete every project in this book. Technique 1 is the easier of the two techniques and is used to make the Triangles Beret on page 6. The Beret is made with two colors, alternating the color with each wedge. You can practice Technique 1 and make the Beret at the same time. See page 6 for the materials needed.

TECHNIQUE 1

This technique places the height of the wedge at the beginning of the rows.

With Tunisian hook, using Taupe and leaving a long end for sewing, chain 17.

Foundation Row (Right side):
📹 Pull up a loop in horizontal bars of the second chain from hook and in each chain across (*Fig. 3*), close: 17 tss.

Fig. 3

Row 1:
Skip the first vertical bar, work tks across to last 2 stitches (15 loops on the hook), leave remaining 2 stitches unworked, close (*Fig. 4*).

Fig. 4

With each row, 2 additional stitches are left unworked.

Rows 2-7:
Skip the first vertical bar, work tks across to last 2 stitches, leave remaining 2 stitches unworked, close: at the end of Row 7, you will have 3 stitches (*Fig. 5*).

Fig. 5

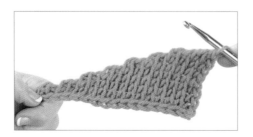

The last row of the wedge (Row 8) smooths out the stair-steps formed by working in short rows. When you come to the last unworked stitch of each row, work into the stitch **below**. This method avoids any gaps that otherwise would be formed.

Row 8:
Skip the first vertical bar, work tks,
📹 work tks in tks one row **below** next st (*Fig. 6*), working in skipped sts across, ★ work tks, work tks in tks one row **below** next tks; repeat from ★ across to last 2 tks, work 2 tks, close
📹 changing to Purple in last st made (*Fig. 21a, page 33*); cut Taupe: 17 tks.

Fig. 6

Turn to page 8 for the instructions to complete the Beret.

TECHNIQUE 2

Now that you've learned Technique 1, you can practice Technique 2 by making the matching Triangles Scarf (see page 9 for the materials needed.

This technique places the height of the wedge at the end of the rows. It requires the use of a split-ring marker, which can easily be placed around a stitch and moved when instructed.

The first wedge of the Triangles Scarf is worked on 15 stitches using Technique 1 and changing colors at the end of Row 7 *(see instructions on page 10)*. The second wedge is worked using Technique 2 as follows:

SECOND WEDGE

Row 1:

Skip the first vertical bar, work 11 tks (12 loops on the hook), place the split-ring marker around last stitch made *(Fig. 7)*, work tks across, close across to the marked stitch; do **not** close remaining stitches.

Fig. 7

The loops will remain on your hook, as you close 2 more stitches on each short row until the wedge is complete.

If you will recall, you ended the first wedge with 3 stitches. For this second wedge, you are beginning with 3 stitches.

Row 2:

Skip first vertical bar, work 2 tks, close across to marked stitch, remove marker, close next 2 stitches, place marker around second loop from hook: 5 tks (11 loops on hook).

When working the third stitch of a short row, work in the stitch **below**. This method avoids any gaps that otherwise would be formed and smooths out the stair-steps formed by working in short rows.

Rows 3-6:

Skip first vertical bar, work tks, work tks in tks one row **below** next tks *(Fig. 8)*, work tks across, close across to marked stitch, remove marker, close next 2 stitches, place marker around second loop from hook; at end of Row 6, do **not** place marker: 13 tks and 3 loops on hook.

Fig. 8

Row 7:

Skip first vertical bar, work tks, work tks in tks one row **below** next tks, work tks across, close across: 15 tks.

Row 8:

Skip first vertical bar, work tks, work tks in tks one row **below** next tks, work tks across to complete the wedge; cut Taupe, with Purple close *(Fig. 21b, page 34)*.

Turn to page 10 for the instructions to complete the Scarf.

Remember, you can watch each technique online!
www.leisurearts.com/5729

triangles
beret

 EASY

Finished Size: 22" (56 cm) circumference at band (unstretched)

SHOPPING LIST

Yarn (Medium Weight) **MEDIUM 4**

[3 ounces, 167 yards (85 grams, 153 meters) per skein]:

☐ Taupe - one skein

☐ Purple - one skein

Hooks

10" (25.5 cm) Tunisian hook,

☐ Size L (8 mm)

or size needed for gauge

Standard crochet hook,

☐ Size F (3.75 mm)

Additional Supplies

☐ Yarn needle

GAUGE INFORMATION

In tks pattern, with Tunisian hook,

11 tks and 13 rows = 4" (10 cm)

In slip st pattern, with standard crochet hook,

7 slip sts = 1" (2.5 cm);

35 rows = 4" (10 cm)

Please refer to gauge on page 31.

The Body is made flat, starting with the top until wedges form a circle. The Band is worked in vertical rows around the circumference of the Body. The Beret is seamed.

INSTRUCTIONS
BODY

With Tunisian hook, using Taupe, and leaving a long end for sewing, ch 17.

See Basic Crochet Stitches, page 31.

Foundation Row (Right side)**:** Pull up a loop in horizontal bar of second ch from hook and each ch across, close: 17 tss.

FIRST WEDGE

Rows 1-7: Skip first vertical bar, work tks across to last 2 sts, leave remaining 2 sts unworked, close: 3 tks.

Row 8: Skip first vertical bar, work tks, work tks in tks one row **below** next tks *(Fig. 6, page 4)*, working in skipped sts across, ★ work tks, work tks in tks one row **below** next tks; repeat from ★ across to last 2 tks, work 2 tks, close changing to Purple in last st made *(Fig. 21a, page 33)*; cut Taupe: 17 tks.

SECOND WEDGE

Rows 1-8: With Purple, repeat Rows 1-8 of First Wedge, changing to Taupe at end of Row 8; cut Purple.

REMAINING 10 WEDGES

Repeat First Wedge and Second Wedge, 5 times; at end of last Wedge, do **not** change colors, do **not** cut Purple.

Bind Off Row: Skip first vertical bar, inserting hook as for tks, 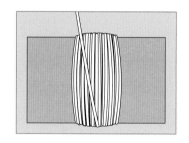 slip st in each st across; finish off.

BAND

Row 1: With **right** side facing and using standard crochet hook, join Purple with slip st in end of Foundation Row; ch 7, slip st in horizontal bar of second ch from hook and in each ch across, slip st in end of next row of Body: 7 slip sts.

If the last stitch of a slip stitch row is too loose, work the last stitch in both loops instead of the Back Loop Only.

Row 2: Turn; slip st in Back Loop Only of each slip st across: 7 slip sts.

Row 3: Turn; slip st in Back Loop Only of first 6 slip sts, skip last slip st, slip st in end of next row on Body: 7 slip sts.

Repeat Rows 2 and 3 across, ending by working Row 2.

Finish off, leaving a long end for sewing.

FINISHING

Thread yarn needle with long end at top of Body. Weave needle through end of rows, gather tightly and secure end; with same yarn, sew First and last Wedges together, working across last row of last Wedge and beginning ch of first Wedge (*Figs. 26a & b, page 35*).

Thread yarn needle with long end from Band and sew last row and beginning ch of Band together.

🎥 POM-POM

Cut a piece of cardboard 3½" (9 cm) square.

Wind Purple around the cardboard until it is approximately ½" (12 mm) thick in the middle (*Fig. 9a*).

Carefully slip the yarn off the cardboard and firmly tie an 18" (45.5 cm) length of yarn around the middle (*Fig. 9b*). Leave yarn ends long enough to attach the pom-pom. Cut the loops on both ends and trim the pom-pom into a smooth ball (*Fig. 9c*).

Attach pom-pom to top of Beret.

Fig. 9a

Fig. 9b

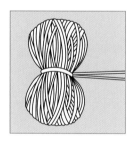

Fig. 9c

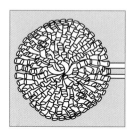

triangles
scarf

 EASY

Finished Size: 6½" wide x 67½" long
(16.5 cm x 171.5 cm)

SHOPPING LIST

Yarn (Medium Weight) 4

**[3 ounces, 167 yards
(85 grams, 153 meters) per skein]:**

☐ Purple - 2 skeins

☐ Taupe - one skein

Hooks

10" (25.5 cm) Tunisian hook,

☐ Size K (6.5 mm)

or size needed for gauge

Standard crochet hook,

☐ Size H (5 mm)

Additional Supplies

☐ Split-ring marker

GAUGE INFORMATION

12 tks and 13 rows = 4" (10 cm)

Please refer to gauge on page 31.

INSTRUCTIONS

The Scarf is formed by alternating colors and Short Row techniques.

BODY

With Tunisian hook and Purple, ch 15.

See Basic Crochet Stitches, page 31.

Foundation Row (Right side): Pull up a loop in horizontal bar of second ch from hook and each ch across, close: 15 tss.

FIRST WEDGE

Rows 1-6: Skip first vertical bar, work tks across to last 2 sts, leave remaining 2 sts unworked, close: 3 tks.

Row 7: Skip first vertical bar, work tks, work tks in tks one row **below** next tks *(Fig. 6, page 4)*, working in skipped sts across, ★ work tks, work tks in tks one row **below** next tks; repeat from ★ across to last 2 tks, work 2 tks, close changing to Taupe in last st made *(Fig. 21a, page 33)*; cut Purple: 15 tks.

SECOND WEDGE

Row 1: Skip first vertical bar, work 11 tks (12 loops on hook), place split-ring marker around last st made *(Fig. 7, page 5)*, work tks across, close across to marked st; do **not** close remaining sts: 3 tks (13 loops on hook).

Row 2: Skip first vertical bar, work 2 tks, close 3 sts, remove marker, close next 2 sts, place marker around second loop from hook: 5 tks (11 loops on hook).

Rows 3-6: Skip first vertical bar, work tks, work tks in tks one row **below** next tks *(Fig. 8, page 5)*, work tks across, close across to marked st, remove marker, close next 2 sts, place marker around second loop from hook; at end of Row 6, do **not** place marker: 13 tks (3 loops on hook).

Row 7: Skip first vertical bar, work tks, work tks in tks one row **below** next tks, work tks across, close: 15 tks.

Row 8: Skip first vertical bar, work tks, work tks in tks one row **below** next tks, work tks across; cut Taupe, with Purple close *(Fig. 21b, page 34)*.

NEXT 41 WEDGES

Repeat First Wedge and Second Wedge, 20 times; then repeat First Wedge once **more**.

LAST WEDGE

Rows 1-6: Repeat Rows 1-6 of Second Wedge: 13 tks (3 loops on hook).

Row 7: Skip first vertical bar, work tks, work tks in tks one row **below** next tks, work tks across, close: 15 tks.

Bind Off Row: Skip first vertical bar, inserting hook as for tks, slip st across; finish off.

TRIM

Rnd 1: With **right** side facing and using standard crochet hook, join Purple with sc in end of Foundation Row; sc evenly around entire Body working 3 sc in each corner; join with slip st to Back Loop Only of first sc.

Rnds 2 and 3: Ch 1, working in Back Loops Only, sc in each sc around working 3 sc in center sc of each corner 3-sc group; join with slip st to Back Loop Only of first sc.

Finish off.

hooded
riding cape

■■□□ **EASY**

Finished Measurements:

Long Vest: 36" (91.5 cm) long

Cape: 19¼" (49 cm) long

Armhole Depth: 9" (23 cm) long

SHOPPING LIST

Yarn (Bulky Weight) 🔵BULKY 5

[3.5 ounces, 120 yards
(100 grams, 110 meters) per hank]:

☐ Long Vest - 12 hanks

☐ Cape - 8 hanks

Hooks

30" (76 cm) Tunisian hook,

☐ Size M (9 mm)

    or size needed for gauge

☐ Standard crochet hooks,

☐ Size J (6 mm) **and**

☐ Size M (9 mm)

Additional Supplies

☐ Split-ring markers - 2

☐ Yarn needle

GAUGE INFORMATION

10 tks and 12 rows = 4" (10 cm)

Please refer to gauge on page 31.

INSTRUCTIONS
Long Vest

The Long Vest is worked in one piece, beginning at one front opening and working across the length of the Vest.

FIRST FRONT

With Tunisian hook, ch 90.

See Basic Crochet Stitches, page 31.

Foundation Row (Right side): Pull up a loop in horizontal bar of second ch from hook and each ch across, close: 90 tss.

Rows 1-3: Skip first vertical bar, work trs across, close: 90 trs.

FIRST WEDGE

Row 1: Skip first vertical bar, work 3 trs, work tks across to last 12 sts, leave remaining 12 sts unworked, close: 78 sts.

Rows 2-13: Skip first vertical bar, work 3 trs, work tks across to last 6 sts, leave remaining 6 sts unworked, close: 6 sts.

Row 14: Skip first vertical bar, work 3 trs, work tks, 📹 work tks in tks one row **below** next tks (*Fig. 6, page 4*), working in skipped sts across, ★ work 5 tks, work tks in tks one row **below** next tks; repeat from ★ across to last 12 tks, work tks across, close: 90 sts.

REMAINING 4 WEDGES

Repeat Rows 1-14, 4 times.

FIRST ARMHOLE SHAPING

Row 1: Skip first vertical bar, work 3 trs, work 62 tks, leave remaining 24 sts unworked, close: 66 sts.

Rows 2-4: Skip first vertical bar, work 3 trs, work tks across, close; do **not** finish off.

BACK

Optional: *Chain Cast On may be used if desired (Figs. 15a & b, page 32).*

Foundation Row: Skip first vertical bar, work 3 trs, work tks across, crochet cast on 24 sts *(Figs 16a-d, page 32)*, close: 90 sts.

FIRST WEDGE

Rows 1-14: Repeat Rows 1-14 of First Wedge of First Front, page 12.

Rows 15-17: Skip first vertical bar, work 3 trs, work tks across, close.

REMAINING 6 WEDGES

Repeat Rows 1-17, 5 times; then repeat Rows 1-14 once **more**.

SECOND ARMHOLE SHAPING

Work same as First Armhole Shaping; do **not** finish off: 66 sts.

SECOND FRONT

Row 1: Skip first vertical bar, work 3 trs, work tks across, cast on 24 sts, close: 90 sts.

NEXT 5 WEDGES

Repeat Rows 1-14 of First Wedge of First Front, 5 times.

Last 2 Rows: Skip first vertical bar, work trs across, close.

Bind Off Row: Skip first vertical bar, inserting hook as for trs, slip st across; finish off.

 Sew shoulders *(Fig. 25, page 34)*.

FRONT TRIM

Row 1: With **right** side facing, using smaller size standard crochet hook, and working across Front opening, join yarn with sc in first trs, sc evenly across Front, Back neck edge, and next Front.

Rows 2-4: Ch 1, turn; sc in each sc across.

Measure 9½" (24 cm) down from shoulder seam on each Front and place split-ring marker around sc on Row 4 for tie placement.

Row 5: Ch 1, turn; ★ sc in each sc across to next marked sc; ch 50, slip st in horizontal bar of second ch from hook and each ch across **(tie made)**; repeat from ★ once **more**, sc in each sc across; finish off.

ARMHOLE TRIM

Rnd 1: With **right** side facing and using smaller size standard crochet hook, join yarn with sc at underarm on either Armhole; sc evenly around; join with slip st to first sc.

Rnds 2 and 3: Ch 1, sc in each sc around; join with slip st to first sc.

Finish off.

Repeat around second Armhole.

Remember, you can watch each technique online!
www.leisurearts.com/5729

Cape

Each row is worked across the length of the Cape, beginning at one front edge and ending at the second front edge. The Hood is added by picking up stitches along the neck edge, working to the top edge and then seaming the last row.

With Tunisian hook, ch 48.

Foundation Row (Right side)**:** Pull up a loop in horizontal bar of second ch from hook and each ch across, close: 48 sts.

Rows 1-3: Skip first vertical bar, work trs across, close: 48 sts.

FIRST WEDGE

Rows 1-7: Skip first vertical bar, work 3 trs, work tks across to last 6 sts, leave remaining 6 sts unworked, close: 6 sts.

Row 8: Skip first vertical bar, work 3 trs, work tks, work tks in tks one row **below** next tks, ★ work 5 tks, work tks in tks one row **below** next tks; repeat from ★ across to last 6 tks, work tks across, close: 48 sts.

REMAINING 31 WEDGES

Repeat Rows 1-7, 31 times.

Last 2 Rows: Skip first vertical bar, work trs across, close: 48 sts.

Bind Off Row: Skip first vertical bar, inserting hook as for trs, slip st across; finish off.

HOOD

Row 1: With **right** side facing, using Tunisian hook, and working in sts across Front opening,  join yarn with slip st in twelfth st from neck edge (**counts as first st**); pick up a loop in remaining 11 sts, pick up 36 loops evenly spaced across end of rows on neck edge, pick up a loop in first 12 sts of next front opening, close: 60 sts.

Row 2: Skip first vertical bar, work tks across, close.

Repeat Row 2 until Hood measures approximately 15" (38 cm).

Finish off, leaving a long end for sewing.

Flatten last row of Hood and  sew top seam (**Figs. 26a & b, page 35**).

FRONT TRIM

Row 1: With **right** side facing, using smaller size standard crochet hook, and working across front opening, join yarn with sc in first trs; sc evenly across Front, Hood, and next Front.

Rows 2-4: Ch 1, turn; sc in each sc across.

Place split-ring marker around each sc on Row 4 at beginning of Hood for tie placement.

Row 5: Ch 1, turn; ★ sc in each sc across to next marked sc; ch 50, slip st in horizontal bar of second ch from hook and each ch across (**tie made**); repeat from ★ once **more**, sc in each sc across; finish off.

puff sleeve cardigan

 INTERMEDIATE

Shown on page 19.

SIZE INFORMATION

Size	Finished Chest Measurement	
Small	32"	(81.5 cm)
Medium	35½"	(90 cm)
Large	39¼"	(99.5 cm)
X-Large	43"	(109 cm)
2X-Large	46½"	(118 cm)

Size Note: We have printed the instructions for the sizes in different colors to make it easier for you to find:
Small in blue
Medium in pink
Large in green
X-Large in purple
2X-Large in red
Instructions in black apply to all sizes.

GAUGE INFORMATION

In Skirt pattern, 10 sts = 4" (10 cm);
   8 rows = 2¾" (7 cm)
   11 tks and 11 rows = 4" (10 cm)
   Please refer to gauge on page 31.

STITCH GUIDE

K2tog (*Fig. 19, page 33*)
Revk2tog (*Fig. 20, page 33*)

The Body is made vertically, then stitches are picked up across the ends of the rows so the Bodice can be worked horizontally. The shoulders are sewn and the sleeves are worked from top down by picking up stitches along the armhole edge.

INSTRUCTIONS
BODY

With Tunisian hook, ch 40.

See Basic Crochet Stitches, page 31.

Foundation Row (Right side): 📹 Pull up a loop in horizontal bar of second ch from hook and each ch across, close: 40 tss.

FIRST WEDGE
Row 1: Skip first vertical bar, work tks, (work trs, work tks) across, close.

Row 2: Skip first vertical bar, work trs, (work tks, work trs) across, close.

Row 3: Skip first vertical bar, work tks, (work trs, work tks) across, close.

Row 4: Skip first vertical bar, work tks across, close.

Rows 5-7: Skip first vertical bar, work tks across to last 10 sts, leave remaining 10 sts unworked, close: 10 tks.

Row 8: Skip first vertical bar, work 8 tks, 📹 work tks in tks one row **below** next tks (*Fig. 6, page 4*), ★ work 9 tks, work tks in tks one row **below** next tks; repeat from ★ across to last 10 tks, work tks across, close: 40 tks.

NEXT {15-17}{19-21-23} WEDGES
Repeat Rows 1-8, {15-17}{19-21-23} times: 40 tks.

Last 3 Rows: Repeat Rows 1-3.

Bind off Row: Skip first vertical bar, inserting hook as for tks, 📹 slip st across; do **not** finish off.

BODICE
Row 1: With **right** side facing and working in end of rows, pick up {84-94}{104-114-124} sts evenly spaced across, close: {85-95}{105-115-125} sts.

Rows 2-4: Skip first vertical bar, work tks across, close.

FIRST FRONT
The Fronts are intentionally longer than the Back, as they include the top of the shoulder.

Row 1: Skip first vertical bar, work {17-19}{22-25-27} tks, leave remaining sts unworked, close: {18-20}{23-26-28} tks.

Rows 2 thru {4-5}{5-6-8}: Skip first vertical bar, work tks across to last 3 sts, revk2tog, work tks in last st, close: {15-16}{19-21-21} tks.

Next {9-8}{10-9-8} Rows: Skip first vertical bar, work tks across, close: {15-16}{19-21-21} tks.

Next Row: Bind off {5-5}{7-9-9} sts, work tks across, close: {10-11}{12-12-12} tks.

Next 3 Rows: Skip first vertical bar, k2tog, work tks across, close: {7-8}{9-9-9} tks.

Next {12-14}{14-14-14} Rows: Skip first vertical bar, work tks across, close.

Bind Off Row: Skip first vertical bar, inserting hook as for tks, slip st across; finish off.

BACK
Row 1: With **right** side facing, skip next 5 sts from Front and 📹 join yarn with slip st in next st (**counts as first st**), work {38-44}{48-52-58} tks, leave remaining sts unworked, close: {39-45}{49-53-59} sts.

Rows 2 thru {3-4}{4-5-7}: Skip first vertical bar, k2tog, work tks across to last 3 sts, revk2tog, work tks in last st, close: {35-39}{43-45-47} sts.

Next {20-21}{23-22-20} Rows: Skip first vertical bar, work tks across, close.

Bind Off Row: Inserting hook as for tks, slip st across; finish off.

SECOND FRONT

Row 1: With **right** side facing, skip next 5 sts from Back and join yarn with slip st in next st (**counts as first st**), work {17-19}{22-25-27} tks, close: {18-20}{23-26-28} sts.

Rows 2 thru {4-5}{5-6-8}: Skip first vertical bar, k2tog, work tks across, close: {15-16}{19-21-21} sts.

Next {9-8}{10-9-8} Rows: Skip first vertical bar, work tks across, close: {15-16}{19-21-21} sts.

Next Row: Skip first vertical bar, work {10-11}{12-12-12} tks, bind off {4-4}{6-8-8} sts, finish off, with new yarn close: {10-11}{12-12-12} sts.

Next 3 Rows: Skip first vertical bar, work tks across to last 3 sts, revk2tog, work tks in last st, close: {7-8}{9-9-9} sts.

Next {12-14}{14-14-14} Rows: Skip first vertical bar, work tks across, close.

Bind off Row: Skip first vertical bar, inserting hook as for tks, slip st across; finish off.

📹 Sew shoulders (*Figs. 26a & b*, *page 35*).

SLEEVE
BODY

The Sleeve is worked from the top down in a join-as-you-go method to reduce seaming. Do not skip the first vertical bar of the row on increase rows.

The stitches of one Sleeve will be picked up from the top row down to the sixth row while the opposite Sleeve's stitches will be picked up from the sixth row up to the top row.

Row 1: With **right** side facing and using Tunisian hook, join yarn with slip st in end of row on Front (**counts as first st**), pull up a loop in end of next 5 rows, close: 6 sts.

Rows 2 thru {18-20}{22-24-27}: Remove loop from hook, insert hook in end of next row down the side of armhole, hook dropped loop and pull loop through side edge, work tks across (including the first vertical bar which is usually skipped), insert hook in end of next row down on opposite side of armhole, pull up a loop, close: {40-44}{48-52-58} sts.

SIZES Small, **Medium**, Large, and **X-Large** ONLY

Next {5-5}{ 5-3} Rows: Remove loop from hook, insert hook in end of next row down the side of armhole, hook dropped loop and pull loop through side edge, skip the first vertical bar, work tks in each st across, remove last loop on hook, insert hook in end of next row down on opposite side of armhole, hook dropped loop and pull loop through side edge, close: {40-44}{48-52} sts.

All SIZES

Next Row: Inserting hook as for tks, slip st in first 3 tks, work tks across to last 2 sts, inserting hook as for tks, slip st in last 2 tks; cut yarn, with new yarn, close: {34-38}{42-46-52} sts.

Next Row: Skip first vertical bar, work tks across, close; do **not** finish off.

RIBBING

Slip loop from Tunisian hook to smaller size standard crochet hook, ch 5.

Row 1: Slip st in horizontal bar of second ch from hook and each ch across, slip st in next st of last row of Sleeve: 5 slip sts.

Row 2: Turn; slip st in  Back Loop Only of each slip st across: 5 slip sts.

Row 3: Turn; slip st in Back Loop Only of first 4 slip sts, skip last slip st, slip st in next st of last row of Sleeve: 5 slip sts.

Repeat Rows 2 and 3 across, ending by working Row 2.

Finish off, leaving a long end for sewing.

Repeat for second Sleeve, beginning on Back.

Thread yarn needle with long end and sew underarm seam.

FINISHING

NECK TRIM
Row 1: With **right** side facing and using larger size standard crochet hook, join yarn with sc in first st on first Front; sc evenly across.

Rows 2 and 3: Ch 1, turn; sc in each sc across.

Finish off.

BUTTON BAND
Row 1: With **right** side facing and using larger size standard crochet hook, join yarn with sc in end of last row on Neck Trim, sc evenly across.

Rows 2-5: Ch 1, turn; sc in each sc across.

Finish off.

BUTTONHOLE BAND
Row 1: With **right** side facing and using larger size standard crochet hook, join yarn with sc in first st on Front; sc evenly across, ending in end of last row on Neck Trim.

Row 2: Ch 1, turn; sc in each sc across.

Place split-ring markers on Row 2 for buttonholes, placing first marker in second sc from neck edge and last marker approximately 10½" (26.5 cm) from bottom edge, evenly spacing markers for remaining {4-4} {5-5-5} buttonholes.

Row 3: Ch 1, turn; sc in each sc across to next marked sc, ch 1, ★ skip marked sc, sc in next sc and in each sc across to next marked sc, ch 1; repeat from ★ across to last marked sc, skip marked sc, sc in last sc.

Row 4: Ch 1, turn; sc in each sc and in each ch-1 sp across.

Row 5: Ch 1, turn; sc in each sc across; finish off.

Sew buttons to Button Band opposite buttonholes.

cobblestone
beanie

◀■■■▭ INTERMEDIATE

Finished Size: 18" (45.5 cm) circumference at band (unstretched)

SHOPPING LIST

Yarn Light Weight Yarn 🔲**3** LIGHT
[1.75 ounces, 153 yards
(50 grams, 140 meters) per skein]:
☐ One skein

Hooks
10" (25.5 cm) Tunisian hook,
☐ Size K (6.5 mm)
  or size needed for gauge
Standard crochet hook,
☐ Size F (3.75 mm)

Additional Supplies
☐ Yarn needle

GAUGE INFORMATION
In stitch pattern (after blocking),
    17 sts and 15.5 rows = 4" (10 cm)
Please refer to gauge on page 31.

——— STITCH GUIDE ———
🎥 Puff Stitch *(Figs. 18a & b, page 33)*

The Body is made flat, starting with the top until wedges form a circle. The Band is worked in vertical rows around the circumference of the Body. The Beanie is seamed. Some rows are written in two parts with the forward pass instructions listed as Step A and the return pass as Step B.

INSTRUCTIONS
BODY
With Tunisian hook and leaving a long end for sewing, ch 26.

See Basic Crochet Stitches, page 31.

Foundation Row (Right side):
Step A: 🎥 Pull up loop in horizontal bar of second ch from hook and each ch across: 26 sts.
Step B: ★ Ch 2, YO and draw through 4 loops on hook; repeat from ★ across to last 2 loops, ch 1, YO and draw through last 2 loops on hook: 8 3-st groups.

FIRST WEDGE

Row 1: Skip first vertical bar, work Puff St in each 3-st group (horizontal bar) across to last 3-st group, pull up a loop in next ch-2 sp, leave remaining sts unworked, close: 23 sts.

Row 2:

Step A: Skip first vertical bar, work tks across to last 3 sts, leave remaining 3 sts unworked: 20 sts.

Step B: ★ Ch 2, YO and draw through 4 loops on hook; repeat from ★ across to last 2 loops, ch 1, YO and draw through 2 loops on hook: 6 3-st groups.

Row 3: Repeat Row 1: 17 sts.

Row 4: Repeat Row 2: Step A -14 sts and Step B - 4 3-st groups.

Row 5: Repeat Row 1: 11 sts.

Row 6: Repeat Row 2: Step A - 8 sts and Step B - 2 3-st groups.

Row 7:

Step A: YO, pull up a loop in ch-1 sp, ★ pull up a loop in horizontal bar of next 3-st group and in next ch-2 sp; repeat from ★ once **more**, work tks in next st; working in skipped sts across, † work 3 tks, pull up a loop in horizontal bar of 3-st group and in next ch-2 sp, work tks in next st †; repeat from † to † 2 times **more**: 26 sts.

Step B: ★ Ch 2, YO and draw through 4 loops on hook; repeat from ★ across to last 2 loops, ch 1, YO and draw through 2 loops on hook: 8 3-st groups.

REMAINING 10 WEDGES

Repeat Rows 1-7, 9 times.

Bind off Row: Skip first vertical bar, inserting hook as for tks, slip st across; finish off.

BAND

Row 1: With **right** side facing and using standard crochet hook, join yarn with slip st in end of Foundation Row; ch 7, slip st in horizontal bar of second ch from hook and in each ch across, slip st in end of next row on Body: 7 slip sts.

Row 2: Turn; slip st in Back Loop Only of each slip st across: 7 slip sts.

Row 3: Turn; slip st in Back Loop Only of first 6 slip sts, skip last slip st, slip st in end of next row on Body: 7 slip sts.

Repeat Rows 2 and 3 across, ending by working Row 2.

Finish off.

Thread yarn needle with beginning long end. Weave needle through end of rows, gather tightly and secure end; with same yarn, sew seam *(Figs. 26a & b, page 35)*.

Remember, you can watch each technique online!
www.leisurearts.com/5729

sapphire wrap

◼◼◼◻ **INTERMEDIATE**

Shown on page 27.

Finished Size: 20" x 76" (51 cm x 193 cm) (after blocking)

SHOPPING LIST

Yarn (Light Weight) **🏷3 LIGHT**
[2.2 ounces, 102 yards
(65 grams, 93 meters) per ball]:
☐ 8 balls

Hook
30" (76 cm) Tunisian hook,
☐ Size K (6.5 mm)
   or size needed for gauge

Additional Supplies
☐ Split-ring marker
☐ Yarn needle

GAUGE INFORMATION

10.5 tks and 15 rows = 4"(10 cm)
   Please refer to gauge on page 31.

──── STITCH GUIDE ────

📹 tds *(Figs. 17a & b, pages 32 & 33)*
📹 Puff St *(Figs. 18a & b, page 33)*
📹 YO *(Fig. 22, page 34)*
📹 M1 *(Fig. 23, page 34)*

The Wrap is worked from the top edge down to the bottom edge. Some rows are written in two parts with the forward pass instructions listed as Step A and the return pass as Step B.

INSTRUCTIONS
WRAP

With Tunisian hook, ch 200.

See Basic Crochet Stitches, page 31.

Foundation Row (Right side): 📹 Pull up a loop in horizontal bar of second ch from hook and each ch across, close: 200 sts.

Rows 1-3: Skip first vertical bar, work trs across, close.

Row 4: Skip first vertical bar, work tks across, close.

FIRST WEDGE

Row 1: Skip first vertical bar, work 95 tks, ▣ place split-ring marker around last st made *(Fig. 7, page 5)*, work tks across to last 4 sts, leave remaining sts unworked, close to marked st.

Row 2: Skip first vertical bar, work tks across to last 4 sts, leave remaining sts unworked, close across to marked st, remove marker, close next 4 sts, place marker around next st.

In each successive short row, the stitches before the marker will decrease by 4 stitches; the stitches after the marker will remain at 100 stitches.

Row 3: Skip first vertical bar, work 3 tks, ▣ work tks in tks one row **below** next tks *(Fig. 6, page 4)*, work tks across to last 4 sts, leave remaining sts unworked, close across to marked st, remove marker, close next 4 sts, place marker around next st.

Rows 4-24: Repeat Row 3, 21 times; at the end of Row 24, do **not** place marker.

Row 25: Skip first vertical bar, work 3 tks, work tks in tks one row **below** next tks, work 94 tks, working in skipped sts across, ▣ work tks in tks one row **below** next tks *(Fig. 8, page 5)* ★ work 3 tks, work tks in one row **below** next tks; repeat from ★ across to last 4 sts, work 4 tks, close: 200 sts.

Row 26: Skip first vertical bar, work 3 tks, work tks in tks one row **below** next tks, work tks across, close.

EYELET SECTION

Row 1:
Step A: Skip first vertical bar, work tks, (skip next vertical bar, work tks) across.
Step B: Ch 2, (YO and draw through 2 loops on hook, ch 1) across to last 3 loops, (YO and draw through 2 loops on hook) twice: 101 sts and 99 ch-1 sps.

Row 2: Skip first vertical bar, work tks, (M1 in next ch-1 sp, work tks in next st) across, close: 200 sts.

SECOND WEDGE

Repeat First Wedge.

EYELET SECTION

Repeat Eyelet Section.

Row 3: Skip first vertical bar, work tks across, close.

LACE TRIM
Row 1:
Step A: Skip first vertical bar, work 2 tks, skip next 2 sts, work 5 tds in next tks, ★ skip next 2 sts, work 4 tks, skip next 2 sts, work 5 tds in next tks; repeat from ★ 20 times **more**, skip next 2 sts, work 3 tks.
Step B: Ch 1, (YO and draw through 2 loops on hook) twice, ch 1, (YO and draw through 2 loops on hook) 5 times, ch 1, ★ (YO and draw through 2 loops on hook) 4 times, ch 1, (YO and draw through 2 loops on hook) 5 times, ch 1; repeat from ★ 20 times **more**, (YO and draw through 2 loops on hook) 3 times.

Row 2:

Step A: Skip first vertical bar, work 2 tks, work Puff St in next 5 tds, ★ work 2 tks, YO, work 2 tks, work Puff St in next 5 tds; repeat from ★ 20 times **more**, work 3 tks.

Step B: Ch 1, (YO and draw through 2 loops on hook) twice, [ch 1, YO and draw through 4 loops on hook (closing 3 loops of Puff St)] 5 times, ch 1, ★ (YO and draw through 2 loops on hook) 5 times, (ch 1, YO and draw through 4 loops on hook) 5 times, ch 1; repeat from ★ 20 times **more**, (YO and draw through 2 loops on hook) 3 times.

Row 3:

Step A: Skip first vertical bar, work 2 tks, skip next ch-1 sp, work Puff St in next 4 ch-1 sps, ★ work 2 tks, YO, M1 in next YO, YO, work 2 tks, skip next ch-1 sp, work Puff St in next 4 ch-1 sps; repeat from ★ 20 times **more**, work 3 tks.

Step B: Ch 1, (YO and draw through 2 loops on hook) twice, (ch 1, YO and draw through 4 loops on hook) 4 times, ch 1, ★ (YO and draw through 2 loops on hook) 7 times, (ch 1, YO and draw through 4 loops on hook) 4 times, ch 1; repeat from ★ 20 times **more**, (YO and draw through 2 loops on hook) 3 times.

Row 4:

Step A: Skip first vertical bar, work 2 tks, skip next ch-1 sp, work Puff St in next 3 ch-1 sps, ★ work 2 tks, M1 in next YO, YO, work tks, YO, M1 in next YO, work 2 tks, skip next ch-1 sp, work Puff St in next 3 ch-1 sps; repeat from ★ 20 times **more**, work 3 tks.

Step B: Ch 1, (YO and draw through 2 loops on hook) twice, (ch 1, YO and draw through 4 loops on hook) 3 times, ch 1, ★ (YO and draw through 2 loops on hook) 9 times, (ch 1, YO and draw through 4 loops on hook) 3 times, ch 1; repeat from ★ 20 times **more**, (YO and draw through 2 loops on hook) 3 times.

Row 5:

Step A: Skip first vertical bar, work 2 tks, skip next ch-1 sp, work Puff St in next 2 ch-1 sps, ★ work 3 tks, M1 in next YO, YO, work tks, YO, M1 in next YO, work 3 tks, skip next ch-1 sp, work Puff St in next 2 ch-1 sps; repeat from ★ 20 times **more**, work 3 tks.

Step B: Ch 1, (YO and draw through 2 loops on hook) twice, (ch 1, YO and draw through 4 loops on hook) twice, ch 1, ★ (YO and draw through 2 loops on hook) 11 times, (ch 1, YO and draw through 4 loops on hook) twice, ch 1; repeat from ★ 20 times **more**, (YO and draw through 2 loops on hook) 3 times.

Row 6:

Step A: Skip first vertical bar, work 2 tks, skip next ch-1 sp, work Puff St in next ch-1 sp, ★ work 4 tks, M1 in next YO, YO, work tks, YO, M1 in next YO, work 4 tks, skip next ch-1 sp, work Puff St in next ch-1 sp; repeat from ★ 20 times **more**, work 3 tks.

Step B: Ch 1, (YO and draw through 2 loops on hook) twice, ch 2, YO and draw through 4 loops on hook, ch 2, ★ (YO and draw through 2 loops on hook) 13 times, ch 2, YO and draw through 4 loops on hook, ch 2; repeat from ★ 20 times **more**, (YO and draw through 2 loops on hook) 3 times.

Row 7:

Step A: Skip first vertical bar, work 2 tks, M1 in next 2 ch-2 sps, ★ work 5 tks, M1 in next YO, YO, work tks, YO, M1 in next YO, work 5 tks, M1 in next 2 ch-2 sps; repeat from ★ 20 times **more**, work 3 tks.

Step B: Ch 1, (YO and draw through 2 loops on hook) twice, ch 1, (YO and draw through 2 loops on hook, ch 1) twice, ★ (YO and draw through 2 loops on hook) 15 times, ch 1, (YO and draw through 2 loops on hook, ch 1) twice; repeat from ★ 20 times **more**, (YO and draw through 2 loops on hook) 3 times; finish off.

general instructions

ABBREVIATIONS

ch(s)	chain(s)
cm	centimeters
k2tog	knit 2 together
M1	make one
mm	millimeters
revk2tog	reverse knit 2 together
Rnd(s)	Round(s)
sc	single crochet(s)
sp(s)	space(s)
st(s)	stitch(es)
tds	Tunisian Double Stitch
tks	Tunisian Knit Stitch
trs	Tunisian Reverse Stitch
YO	yarn over

SYMBOLS & TERMS

★ — work instructions following ★ as many **more** times as indicated in addition to the first time.

† to † — work all instructions from first † to second † **as many** times as specified.

( ) or [ ] — work enclosed instructions **as many** times as specified by the number immediately following **or** work all enclosed instructions in the stitch or space indicated **or** contains explanatory remarks.

colon (:) — the number(s) given after a colon at the end of a row or round denote(s) the number of stitches you should have on that row or round.

CROCHET TERMINOLOGY	
UNITED STATES	**INTERNATIONAL**
slip stitch (slip st) =	single crochet (sc)
single crochet (sc) =	double crochet (dc)
half double crochet (hdc) =	half treble crochet (htr)
double crochet (dc) =	treble crochet(tr)
treble crochet (tr) =	double treble crochet (dtr)
double treble crochet (dtr) =	triple treble crochet (ttr)
triple treble crochet (tr tr) =	quadruple treble crochet (qtr)
skip =	miss

■□□□ BEGINNER	Projects for first-time crocheters using basic stitches. Minimal shaping.	
■■□□ EASY	Projects using yarn with basic stitches, repetitive stitch patterns, simple color changes, and simple shaping and finishing.	
■■■□ INTERMEDIATE	Projects using a variety of techniques, such as basic lace patterns or color patterns, mid-level shaping and finishing.	
■■■■ EXPERIENCED	Projects with intricate stitch patterns, techniques and dimension, such as non-repeating patterns, multi-color techniques, fine threads, small hooks, detailed shaping and refined finishing.	

Yarn Weight Symbol & Names	LACE 0	SUPER FINE 1	FINE 2	LIGHT 3	MEDIUM 4	BULKY 5	SUPER BULKY 6
Type of Yarns in Category	Fingering, 10-count crochet thread	Sock, Fingering Baby	Sport, Baby	DK, Light Worsted	Worsted, Afghan, Aran	Chunky, Craft, Rug	Bulky, Roving
Crochet Gauge* Ranges in Single Crochet to 4" (10 cm)	32-42 double crochets**	21-32 sts	16-20 sts	12-17 sts	11-14 sts	8-11 sts	5-9 sts
Advised Hook Size Range	Steel*** 6,7,8 Regular hook B-1	B-1 to E-4	E-4 to 7	7 to I-9	I-9 to K-10.5	K-10.5 to M-13	M-13 and larger

*GUIDELINES ONLY: The chart above reflects the most commonly used gauges and hook sizes for specific yarn categories.

** Lace weight yarns are usually crocheted on larger-size hooks to create lacy openwork patterns. Accordingly, a gauge range is difficult to determine. Always follow the gauge stated in your pattern.

*** Steel crochet hooks are sized differently from regular hooks–the higher the number the smaller the hook, which is the reverse of regular hook sizing.

GAUGE

Exact gauge is essential for proper size. Before beginning your project, make a sample swatch in the yarn and hook specified in the individual instructions. After completing the swatch, measure it, counting your stitches and rows carefully. If your swatch is larger or smaller than specified, **make another, changing hook size to get the correct gauge.** Keep trying until you find the size hook that will give you the specified gauge.

BASIC CROCHET STITCHES
JOINING WITH SC

When instructed to join with sc, begin with a slip knot on hook. Insert hook in stitch or space indicated, YO and pull up a loop, YO and draw through both loops on hook.

BACK RIDGE (horizontal bar)

Work only in loop indicated by arrow (*Fig. 10*).

Fig. 10

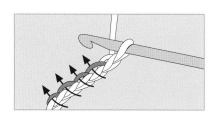

BACK LOOP ONLY

Work only in loop(s) indicated by arrow (*Fig. 11*).

Fig. 11

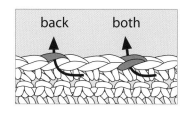

FREE LOOPS OF A CHAIN

When instructed to work in free loops of a chain, work in loops indicated by arrow (*Fig. 12*).

Fig. 12

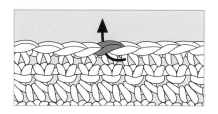

SLIP STITCH (abbreviated slip st)

Insert hook in stitch indicated, YO and draw through st and through loop on hook (*Fig. 13*).

Fig. 13

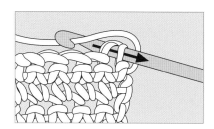

SINGLE CROCHET
(abbreviated sc)

Insert hook in stitch indicated, YO and pull up a loop, YO and draw through both loops on hook (*Fig. 14*).

Fig. 14

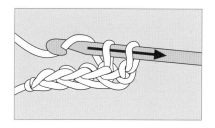

CROCHET HOOKS															
U.S.	B-1	C-2	D-3	E-4	F-5	G-6	H-8	I-9	J-10	K-10½	L-11	M/N-13	N/P-15	P/Q	Q	S
Metric - mm	2.25	2.75	3.25	3.5	3.75	4	5	5.5	6	6.5	8	9	10	15	16	19

CHAIN CAST ON

Using a separate ball of yarn and a standard crochet hook, chain the specified number and join the chain with slip st to the side edge of the last stitch of the row *(Fig. 15a)*; finish off. Continuing with Tunisian hook, pull up a loop in horizontal bar of each ch across *(Fig. 15b)*.

Fig. 15a

Fig. 15b

CROCHET CAST ON

Once the forward pass of a row is completed, turn the work so the **wrong** side is facing you.

Insert standard crochet hook under the front vertical bar of the last stitch made, yarn over and pull up a loop *(Fig. 16a)*.

Fig. 16a

To ch 1 around the Tunisian hook, move the yarn toward you and under the Tunisian hook so that it is again positioned behind the Tunisian hook *(Fig. 16b)*, ch 1.

Fig. 16b

The first cast on stitch is made *(Fig. 16c)*.

Fig. 16c

Repeat this process until you have completed all but the last cast on st required.

Place the loop from the standard hook onto the Tunisian hook *(Fig. 16d)*.

Fig. 16d

TUNISIAN CROCHET STITCHES
TUNISIAN DOUBLE STITCH
(abbreviated tds)

YO, insert hook from the **front** to the **back** between the front and back vertical bars of stitch indicated, YO and pull up a loop, YO and draw through 2 loops on hook *(Figs. 17a & b)*.

Fig. 17a

Fig. 17b

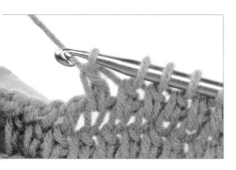

TUNISIAN PUFF STITCH

(abbreviated Puff st)

Insert the hook in the stitch or space indicated *(Fig. 18a)*, YO and pull up a loop (**first stitch**), YO (**second stitch**), insert hook in the same stitch or space, YO and pull up a loop (**third stitch**) *(Fig. 18b)*.

Fig. 18a

Fig. 18b

KNIT 2 TOGETHER

(abbreviated k2tog)

Insert hook from the **front** to the **back** between the front and back vertical bars of the next 2 stitches *(Fig. 19)*. Yarn over and pull the loop through to decrease one stitch.

Fig. 19

REVERSE KNIT 2 TOGETHER

(abbreviated revk2tog)

Skip one stitch, using hook, pull the front vertical bar of next stitch until it is on top of the skipped stitch *(Fig. 20)*, then insert the hook from the **front** to the **back** between vertical bars of both stitches, yarn over and pull the loop through to decrease one stitch.

Fig. 20

Gently stretching the stitches and holding the skipped stitch flat with non-hook hand may help in making the decrease. Then pull the next stitch over the skipped stitch.

ADDING NEW BALL OF YARN OR CHANGING COLORS

It is best to add a new ball of yarn at the end or beginning of a row. By adding at end of a row, the yarn will end up at a seam and will not be visible on the finished piece.

To change colors at the beginning of a row, close the stitches until 2 loops remain on the hook. Drop the old yarn and with the new yarn *(Fig. 21a)*, yarn over and draw through 2 loops on the hook. Be sure to leave at least a 6" (15 cm) end to weave in later.

Fig. 21a

33

To change colors at the end of the row, once you have completed all the stitches but before closing, drop the old yarn, yarn over and pull through one loop *(Fig. 21b)*, then close as usual: one loop. Be sure to leave at least a 6" (15 cm) end to weave in later.

Fig. 21b

YARN OVER *(abbreviated YO)*

A yarn over is simply that, made by either placing the hook under the yarn or by wrapping the yarn from **front** to **back** over the hook. It creates a "hole" or "eyelet," *(Fig. 22)* and increases the number of stitches by one stitch.

Fig. 22

MAKE ONE *(abbreviated M1)*

A Make One is executed by inserting the hook from front to back under the "yarn over" created in the previous row *(Fig. 23)* **or** in the space indicated, then YO and pull up a loop to increase the number of stitches by one stitch.

Fig. 23

COUNTING THE ROWS

It is easiest to count your rows along the side edge at the beginning of the rows *(Fig. 24)*.

Fig. 24

SEAMING

When seaming along the ends of the rows, use the yarn needle to go under the 2 bars of the Tunisian Knit Stitches on each side *(Fig. 25)*. Try not to pull the seaming stitches too tightly as this will cause the fabric to buckle. You want your rows to "sit together" next to each other as though they are within the row.

Fig. 25

Remember, you can watch each technique online!
www.leisurearts.com/5729

When seaming across the last row, use the needle in the same manner, to go under the 2 bars of the Tunisian Knit Stitches *(Figs. 26a & b)*. This will cause the chain to be pushed to the **wrong** side of the work.

Fig. 26a

Fig. 26b

BLOCKING

Blocking helps to smooth your work and give it a professional appearance. You may block your work while it is in separate pieces for easier assembly.

With acrylics that can be blocked, simply pin the piece to the correct size with rust-proof pins and cover it with dampened bath towels. When the towels are dry, the piece is blocked.

If the piece is hand washable, carefully launder it using a mild soap or detergent. Rinse it without wringing or twisting. Remove any excess moisture by rolling it in a succession of dry towels. You can put it in the final spin cycle of your washer, without water.

Lay the piece on a large towel on a flat surface out of direct sunlight. Using a tape measure, gently smooth and pat it to the desired size and shape. When it is completely dry, it is blocked.

Another method of blocking that is for wool or wool blends requires a steam iron or hand steamer. With the wrong side of the piece facing, pin it out with rust-proof pins to the correct size. Hold the iron or steamer just above the piece and steam thoroughly. Never let the weight of the iron or steamer touch the piece as it will flatten the stitches. Leave cables, ribbings, or intricate raised patterns unsteamed. Leave the piece pinned until it is completely dry.

KIM GUZMAN fills each day with creativity. Whether she's knitting or crocheting a new design or working on a new canning experiment with the fruit and vegetables she grows at home in Arkansas, she fulfills a lifelong dream—endless creative ventures in a lovely country setting with her family close at hand.

The design work that helps Kim realize this dream has won several awards, including three 2010 "Flamies" from the Crochet Liberation Front. There are several books of her patterns, and her designs have appeared in popular yarn craft magazines.

Kim says, "Like in hand-knitting, you can create short rows with Tunisian crochet. I find using short rows to be fun and addictive. Because your rows are constantly changing, it doesn't get monotonous and projects seem to fly off the hook in no time at all. There is nothing mysterious about short rows. You are simply working stitches across a row, decreasing at the end, making fewer and fewer stitches until that portion is complete. Then, you repeat the process. Very fun!"

Learn more about Kim and her creations at KimaneDesigns.net and CrochetKim.com. She also has a Ravelry.com page and a blog called WIPs 'N Chains at KimGuzman.wordpress.com.

yarn
information

The items in this book were made using a variety of yarns. Any brand of the specified weight of yarn may be used. It is best to refer to the yardage/meters when determining how many balls or skeins to purchase. Remember, to arrive at the finished size, it is the GAUGE/TENSION that is important, not the brand of yarn.

For your convenience, listed below are the specific yarns used to create our photography models.

TRIANGLES BERET
Vickie Howell Sheep(ish)
#0011 Taupe(ish)
#0006 Magenta(ish)

TRIANGLES SCARF
Vickie Howell Sheep(ish)
#0011 Taupe(ish)
#0006 Magenta(ish)

HOODED RIDING CAPE
Universal Yarn Deluxe Chunky
#91476 Fire Red

PUFF SLEEVE CARDIGAN
Red Heart® Boutique™ Eclipse™
#9801 Storm Blue

COBBLESTONE BEANIE
Fibra Natura® Cobblestone
#308 Rodeo Drive

SAPPHIRE WRAP
Patons® Silk Bamboo
#85134 Royal

We have made every effort to ensure that these instructions are accurate and complete. We cannot, however, be responsible for human error, typographical mistakes, or variations in individual work.

Production Team: Writer/Technical Editor - Lois J. Long; Editorial Writer - Susan McManus Johnson; Senior Graphic Artist - Lora Puls; Graphic Artists - Jacob Casleton and Katherine Laughlin; Photo Stylist - Brooke Duszota; and Photographer - Jason Masters.